IN
COURAGE
Journal

IN
COU

A Daily Practice for Self-Discovery

RAGE

Journal

ALEXANDRA ELLE

CHRONICLE BOOKS

SAN FRANCISCO

ISBN: 978-1-7972-0011-8

Manufactured in China.

Design by Vanessa Dina.

10 9 8 7 6 5 4 3 2

Chronicle books and gifts are available at special quantity discounts to
corporations, professional associations, literacy programs, and other
organizations. For details and discount information, please contact our premiums
department at corporatesales@chroniclebooks.com or at 1-800-759-0190.

Chronicle Books LLC
680 Second Street
San Francisco, California 94107
www.chroniclebooks.com

DEAR WRITER,

Welcome to *In Courage*. This journal was crafted
as a tool for diving deeper into a personal relationship with the stories you carry—a companion
for exploring your inner voice through introspective writing practice. Journaling became a
pivotal tool for me in my teen years. It helped
shape and mold my voice as I went through
the ebbs and flows of everyday life. Writing in
my journal over the years has taught me to be
honest in new ways. It's given me the self-trust
and courage to sort out my emotions, feelings,
and ideas. Through the years, I've grown to love
guided journaling and how it prompts me to be
introspective. I created *In Courage* to help those of
us who struggle with blank-page journaling and
to bring forth new ways of thinking about life,
healing, and self-care.

These pages will guide you closer to your
purpose—whatever that may be. It's no easy feat
to show up fully, reflect on lessons learned, and

find new ways to use your voice on and off the page. My hope is that you'll finish this journal with a better grasp on finding affirming language and using creativity to get to know yourself better. I designed *In Courage* to be easy, functional, and accessible for all who long to manifest a closer relationship with themselves. When I'm teaching writing workshops, I often hear people say journaling is "challenging," "intimidating," or "scary." Those same people tell me, "I'm not a writer. I don't know what to say." If you're one of those people, *In Courage* can help you dispel that myth. You can do this. Everyone can write! You don't need to be an expert or a scholar to journal. The goal is to approach the pages with honesty and self-love rooted in the pursuit of learning a lesson or discovering a new one. The intention behind this journal is to get you ready, excited, and confident for a journey through daily writing and authentic inner dialog.

In Courage is a daily journaling practice organized into morning and evening writing prompts. The prompts are designed to help you implement self-care and self-love in your life. I found that starting and ending my day with journaling allows me to be more present and in tune with myself. It sets the tone for how I rise in the morning and settle down for the night. There are also gentle reminders to support you on your journey, short prompts to encourage creative writing, and drawing prompts to help you explore your inner world. Be honest in your writing practice, and don't think too hard. This is a safe space for self-discovery. Let the words flow.

Have fun with this! There's no right or wrong way to show up on the page. Do your best. Cherish it. And don't be too hard on yourself. This tool is yours to make a mess in or keep clean. Your writing creates encapsulated moments in time. Someday, you'll look back through this journal and say, "Wow, look how far I've come." Express yourself on the pages in a way that feels good and encourages your personal writing practice and process. Use your favorite pen, get in a comfortable seat, and start your mornings and wrap up your nights with words that facilitate your ability to recharge, reflect, and reshape your narrative.

Thank you for being here and choosing *In Courage* as your guide to a better version of yourself!

Big love,
ALEX ELLE

Morning

Today is a new day to learn:

_____

_____

_____

I am: _____

I will: _____

I can: _____

My self-love practice for the day is:

_____

_____

_____

I will stand in courage today by:

_____

_____

_____

Evening

Today I learned:

_____

_____

_____

I expect: _____

I need: _____

I deserve: _____

I showed myself love and compassion today by:

_____

_____

_____

Today's acts of courage:

1. _____

2. _____

3. _____

Morning

Today is a new day to learn:

_____

_____

_____

I am: _____

I will: _____

I can: _____

How can I open my heart to forgiveness?

_____

_____

_____

I will stand in courage today by:

_____

_____

_____

Evening

Today I learned:

I expect:

I need:

I deserve:

I forgive myself for:

I forgive them for:

Today's acts of courage:

1.

2.

3.

Self-love won't develop overnight. I am dedicated to practicing it daily and starting over if I need to without shame or self-judgment.

Morning

Today is a new day to learn:

_____

_____

_____

I am: _____

I will: _____

I can: _____

My healing is showing me how to:

_____

_____

_____

I will stand in courage today by:

_____

_____

_____

Evening

Despite the storms I face, I will:

_____

_____

_____

I am preparing for joy by:

_____

_____

_____

_____

Through adversity, I will continue to learn:

_____

_____

_____

_____

_____

Morning

Today is a new day to learn:

_____

_____

_____

I am: _____

I will: _____

I can: _____

Self-soothing intention for the day:

_____

_____

I will stand in courage today by:

_____

_____

_____

_____

Evening

Today I learned:

_____

_____

_____

I expect: _____

I need: _____

I deserve: _____

I showed myself love and compassion today by:

_____

_____

Today's acts of courage:

1. _____

2. _____

3. _____

I will leave behind anything that is weighing me down and hindering my process of unfolding into my best and most authentic self.

Draw

Self-love is teaching me:

Morning

Today is a new day to learn:

_____

_____

_____

I am: _____

I belong: _____

I can: _____

Self-care practices for the day:

1. _____

2. _____

3. _____

I will stand in courage today by:

_____

_____

_____

Evening

Today I learned:

_____

_____

_____

I expect: _____

I need: _____

I deserve: _____

I practiced self-validation by:

_____

_____

_____

Today's acts of courage:

1. _____

2. _____

3. _____

Morning

Today is a new day to learn:

_____

_____

_____

I am: _____

I create: _____

I can: _____

Who am I becoming?

_____

_____

_____

I will stand in courage today by:

_____

_____

_____

Evening

Today I learned:

_____

_____

_____

I expect: _____

I need: _____

I deserve: _____

Each day, with practice, I am becoming:

_____

_____

_____

Today's acts of courage:

1. _____

2. _____

3. _____

I am standing tall and fearless in my truth as I move through my life and learn my worth. I can validate my own story.

Morning

Today is a new day to learn:

_____

_____

_____

I am: _____

I will: _____

I can: _____

What does family look like in my life today?

_____

_____

_____

I will stand in courage today by:

_____

_____

_____

Evening

Today I learned:

_____

_____

_____

I expect: _____

I need: _____

I deserve: _____

Family teaches me to lean into:

_____

_____

_____

Today's acts of courage:

1. _____

2. _____

3. _____

Morning

Today is a new day to learn:

_____

_____

_____

I am: _____

I will: _____

I can: _____

My healing is showing me how to:

_____

_____

_____

I will stand in courage today by:

_____

_____

_____

Evening

Despite the storms I face, I will:

I am preparing for joy by:

Through adversity, I will continue to learn:

Write a Poem

Healing is teaching me:

Forgiveness
has the ability
to set me free
and make me
whole.

Make a List

I am soothing my suffering by:

Morning

Today is a new day to learn:

_____

_____

_____

I am: _____

I will: _____

I can: _____

Who am I today?

_____

_____

_____

I will stand in courage today by:

_____

_____

_____

Evening

Today I learned:

_____

_____

_____

I expect: _____

I need: _____

I deserve: _____

I showed myself love and compassion today by:

_____

_____

_____

Today's acts of courage:

1. _____

2. _____

3. _____

Morning

Today is a new day to learn:

_____

_____

_____

I am: _____

I will: _____

I can: _____

Taking time to breathe and heal feels like:

_____

_____

_____

I will stand in courage today by:

_____

_____

_____

Evening

Today I learned:

_____

_____

_____

I expect: _____

I need: _____

I deserve: _____

Today, I took my time focusing on:

_____

_____

_____

Today's acts of courage:

1. _____

2. _____

3. _____

I am learning how to face my grief when it comes to the surface. I am growing daily.

Morning

Today is a new day to learn:

_____

_____

_____

I am: _____

I will: _____

I can: _____

What I have lost doesn't define my:

_____

_____

_____

I will stand in courage today by:

_____

_____

_____

Evening

Today I learned:

I expect:

I need:

I deserve:

I am holding space for feelings of loss by:

Today's acts of courage:

1.

2.

3.

DATE:

Morning

Today is a new day to learn:

I am:

I will:

I can:

My healing is showing me how to:

I will stand in courage today by:

Evening

Today I learned:

_____

_____

_____

I expect: _____

I need: _____

I deserve: _____

I am creating a pathway to healing by:

_____

_____

_____

Today's acts of courage:

1. _____

2. _____

3. _____

I am finding a
new sense of
family from
the community
around me.

Write a Poem

Validation is teaching me:

Morning

Today is a new day to learn:

I am:

I will:

I can:

My grief has helped me understand:

I will stand in courage today by:

Evening

Today I learned:

I expect:

I need:

I deserve:

I acknowledged my grief today by:

Today's acts of courage:

1.

2.

3.

Morning

Today is a new day to learn:

_____

_____

_____

I am: _____

I will: _____

I can: _____

Love makes me feel:

_____

_____

_____

I will stand in courage today by:

_____

_____

_____

Evening

Today I learned:

I expect:

I need:

I deserve:

I witnessed/experienced love today in:

Today's acts of courage:

1.

2.

3.

Learning lessons
from the mistakes
I make creates
space for greater
understanding.

Morning

Today is a new day to learn:

_____

_____

_____

I am: _____

I will: _____

I can: _____

My ability to change is shaping:

_____

_____

_____

I will stand in courage today by:

_____

_____

_____

Evening

Today I learned:

I expect:

I need:

I deserve:

My evolution has helped me:

Today's acts of courage:

1.

2.

3.

Morning

Today is a new day to learn:

_____

_____

_____

I am: _____

I will: _____

I can: _____

What am I no longer willing to accept?

_____

_____

_____

I will stand in courage today by:

_____

_____

_____

Evening

Today I learned:

_____

_____

_____

I expect: _____

I need: _____

I deserve: _____

What truth do I accept about myself?

_____

_____

_____

Today's acts of courage:

1. _____

2. _____

3. _____

I am in a season
of acceptance and
understanding.
I am doing my best.

Draw

Becoming is teaching me:

Morning

Today is a new day to learn:

_____

_____

_____

I am: _____

I will: _____

I can: _____

How can I open my heart to forgiveness?

_____

_____

_____

I will stand in courage today by:

_____

_____

_____

Evening

Today I learned:

_____

_____

_____

I expect: _____

I need: _____

I deserve: _____

I forgive myself for: _____

I forgive them for: _____

_____

Today's acts of courage:

1. _____

2. _____

3. _____

Morning

Today is a new day to learn:

_____

_____

_____

I am: _____

I will: _____

I can: _____

My time is valuable because:

_____

_____

_____

I will stand in courage today by:

_____

_____

_____

Evening

Today I learned:

I expect:

I need:

I deserve:

I am making more time for things that:

Today's acts of courage:

1.

2.

3.

I trust in my ability to change and give myself grace through the process.

Morning

Today is a new day to learn:

_____

_____

_____

I am: _____

I will: _____

I can: _____

Self-soothing intention for the day:

_____

_____

_____

I will stand in courage today by:

_____

_____

_____

Evening

Today I learned:

I deserve:

I expect:

I need:

Despite the storms I will face, I will:

I am preparing for joy by:

Through adversity, I will continue to learn:

Morning

Today is a new day to learn:

_____

_____

_____

I am: _____

I will: _____

I can: _____

My self-love practice for the day is:

_____

_____

_____

I will stand in courage today by:

_____

_____

_____

Evening

Today I learned:

_____

_____

_____

I expect: _____

I need: _____

I deserve: _____

I showed myself love and compassion today by:

_____

_____

_____

Today's acts of courage:

1. _____

2. _____

3. _____

Loss is teaching me to appreciate what I have and prepare for joy.

Make a List

Family is teaching me:

Morning

Today is a new day to learn:

_____

_____

_____

I am: _____

I will: _____

I can: _____

How can I open my heart to forgiveness?

_____

_____

I will stand in courage today by:

_____

_____

_____

Evening

Today I learned:

_____

_____

_____

I expect: _____

I need: _____

I deserve: _____

I forgive myself for: _____

I forgive them for: _____

_____

Today's acts of courage:

1. _____

2. _____

3. _____

Morning

Today is a new day to learn:

_____

_____

_____

I am: _____

I will: _____

I can: _____

My healing is showing me how to:

_____

_____

_____

I will stand in courage today by:

_____

_____

_____

Evening

Despite the storms I face, I will:

_____

_____

_____

I am preparing for joy by:

_____

_____

_____

Through adversity, I will continue to learn:

_____

_____

_____

_____

_____

I am learning
how to bravely
trust my voice.

Morning

Today is a new day to learn:

_____

_____

_____

I am: _____

I will: _____

I can: _____

Self-soothing intention for the day:

_____

_____

_____

I will stand in courage today by:

_____

_____

_____

Evening

Today I learned:

I expect:

I need:

I deserve:

I showed myself love and compassion today by:

Today's acts of courage:

1.

2.

3.

Draw

Grief is teaching me:

Morning

Today is a new day to learn:

_____

_____

_____

I am: _____

I belong: _____

I can: _____

Self-care practices for the day:

1. _____

2. _____

3. _____

I will stand in courage today by:

_____

_____

_____

Evening

Today I learned:

_____

_____

_____

I expect: _____

I need: _____

I deserve: _____

I practiced self-validation by:

_____

_____

_____

Today's acts of courage:

1. _____

2. _____

3. _____

Change continues
to shape me in
the best ways,
even when it's
uncomfortable.

Write a Poem

Identity is teaching me:

Morning

Today is a new day to learn:

I am:

I create:

I can:

Who am I becoming?

I will stand in courage today by:

Evening

Today I learned:

_____

_____

_____

I expect: _____

I need: _____

I deserve: _____

Each day, with practice, I am becoming:

_____

_____

_____

Today's acts of courage:

1. _____

2. _____

3. _____

Morning

Today is a new day to learn:

_____

_____

_____

I am: _____

I will: _____

I can: _____

What does family look like in my life today?

_____

_____

_____

I will stand in courage today by:

_____

_____

_____

Evening

Today I learned:

I expect:

I need:

I deserve:

Family teaches me to lean into:

Today's acts of courage:

1.

2.

3.

Write a Poem

Change is teaching me:

I am learning how to courageously mend, heal, and soothe the tender parts of my story.

Morning

Today is a new day to learn:

_____

_____

_____

I am: _____

I will: _____

I can: _____

My healing is showing me how to:

_____

_____

_____

I will stand in courage today by:

_____

_____

_____

Evening

Despite the storms I face, I will:

I am preparing for joy by:

Through adversity, I will continue to learn:

Morning

Today is a new day to learn:

_____

_____

_____

I am: _____

I will: _____

I can: _____

Who am I today?

_____

_____

_____

I will stand in courage today by:

_____

_____

_____

Evening

Today I learned:

_____

_____

_____

I expect: _____

I need: _____

I deserve: _____

I showed myself love and compassion today by:

_____

_____

_____

Today's acts of courage:

1. _____

2. _____

3. _____

Healing isn't a
linear process.
I am taking
my time and
mending slowly.

Draw

Learning to breathe is teaching me:

Time is a great teacher. I am learning from each passing minute.

Morning

Today is a new day to learn:

_____

_____

_____

I am: _____

I will: _____

I can: _____

Taking time to breathe and heal feels like:

_____

_____

_____

I will stand in courage today by:

_____

_____

_____

Evening

Today I learned:

_____

_____

_____

I expect: _____

I need: _____

I deserve: _____

Today, I took my time focusing on:

_____

_____

_____

Today's acts of courage:

1. _____

2. _____

3. _____

Morning

Today is a new day to learn:

_____

_____

_____

I am: _____

I will: _____

I can: _____

What I have lost doesn't define my:

_____

_____

_____

I will stand in courage today by:

_____

_____

_____

DATE:

Evening

Today I learned:

I expect:

I need:

I deserve:

I am holding space for feelings of loss by:

Today's acts of courage:

1.

2.

3.

Each new day,
I am becoming
my best self.

Morning

Today is a new day to learn:

_____

_____

_____

I am: _____

I will: _____

I can: _____

My healing is showing me how to:

_____

_____

_____

I will stand in courage today by:

_____

_____

_____

Evening

Today I learned:

_____

_____

_____

I expect: _____

I need: _____

I deserve: _____

I am creating a pathway to healing by:

_____

_____

_____

Today's acts of courage:

1. _____

2. _____

3. _____

Draw

Acceptance is teaching me:

Morning

Today is a new day to learn:

_____

_____

_____

I am: _____

I will: _____

I can: _____

My grief has helped me understand:

_____

_____

_____

I will stand in courage today by:

_____

_____

_____

Evening

Today I learned:

I expect:

I need:

I deserve:

I acknowledged my grief today by:

Today's acts of courage:

1.

2.

3.

I am proud of
who I am and
what I have to
offer the world,
even when others
don't understand.

Morning

Today is a new day to learn:

_____
_____
_____

I am: _____

I will: _____

I can: _____

My healing is showing me how to:

_____
_____
_____

I will stand in courage today by:

_____
_____
_____

Evening

Despite the storms I face, I will:

_____

_____

_____

I am preparing for joy by:

_____

_____

_____

Through adversity, I will continue to learn:

_____

_____

_____

_____

_____

Write a Poem

Time is teaching me:

Morning

Today is a new day to learn:

_____

_____

_____

I am: _____

I will: _____

I can: _____

Who am I today?

_____

_____

_____

I will stand in courage today by:

_____

_____

_____

Evening

Today I learned:

_____

_____

_____

I expect:

I need: _____

I deserve: _____

I showed myself love and compassion today by:

_____

_____

_____

Today's acts of courage:

1. _____

2. _____

3. _____

Love has the power to fill me up in more ways than one. I am grateful and open to love in all its forms.

Morning

Today is a new day to learn:

_____

_____

_____

I am: _____

I will: _____

I can: _____

Taking time to breathe and heal feels like:

_____

_____

_____

I will stand in courage today by:

_____

_____

_____

Evening

Today I learned:

I expect:

I need:

I deserve:

Today, I took my time focusing on:

Today's acts of courage:

1.

2.

3.

Make a List

Forgiveness is teaching me:

Inhale lessons,
exhale regrets.
Learn from it all.

Ryan Spearman

ALEXANDRA ELLE is a writer, a poet, and the author of *After the Rain*. She teaches workshops on writing, self-discovery, and self-care throughout the world. She lives outside Washington, DC.